SOUTH SHIELDS

THE POSTCARD COLLECTION

Caroline Barnsley

AMBERLEY

WOULDHAVE MEMORIAL.
FROM SOUTH SHIELD PARK.

For Dave and Harry, for their constant support and belief.

First published 2014

Amberley Publishing
The Hill, Stroud, Gloucestershire, GL5 4EP
www.amberley-books.com

Copyright © Caroline Barnsley, 2014

The right of Caroline Barnsley to be identified as the
Author of this work has been asserted in accordance with
the Copyrights, Designs and Patents Act 1988.

ISBN 978 1 4456 3446 3 (print)
ISBN 978 1 4456 3454 8 (ebook)

British Library Cataloguing in Publication Data.
A catalogue record for this book is available from the
British Library.

Typesetting by Amberley Publishing.
Printed in Great Britain.

CONTENTS

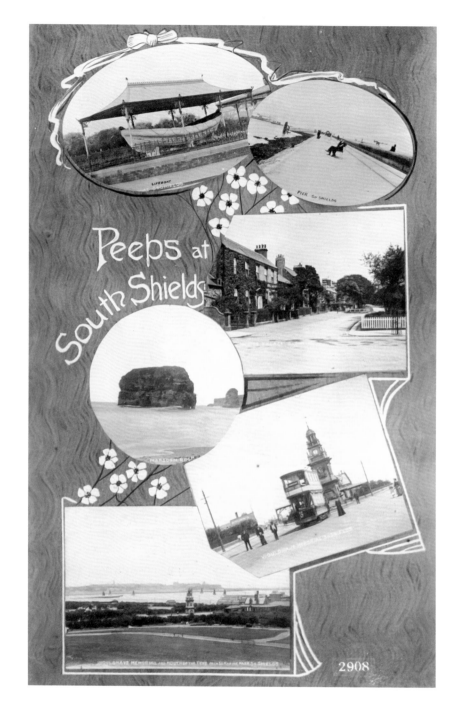

Peeps at South Shields

2908

INTRODUCTION

Caroline Barnsley has produced a remarkable snapshot of life in South Shields over a period of almost 150 years, offering an important perspective into the town's history. With so much material available from her personal archive, Caroline's greatest challenge must have been the selection of appropriate material, but she has cleverly sequenced the postcards to tell a fascinating story, enhanced by a detailed supporting text.

Caroline's work confounds the common impression that South Shields is an industrial town that declined with shipbuilding and mining. In fact, over the centuries other industries, such as salt extraction and glassmaking, expanded and contracted, while South Shields prospered through its proud maritime heritage, which still resonates in the centre of worldwide nautical excellence at South Tyneside College. Caroline depicts wealthy nineteenth-century merchants watching ships entering the River Tyne from their vantage points in Westoe Village, on the very route of the 'Salter's Trod', which had been followed by medieval merchants transporting salt panned on the Tyne. Her postcards offer spectacular views of the harbour and a range of ships on the Tyne in fine weather, but the postcards of the Lifeguard Station and Wouldhave Memorial also help to illustrate the many tragedies that befell seamen at the mouth of the river and in coastal waters.

South Shields enjoys a magnificent location on the North Sea coast, and Caroline gives a clear insight into South Shields as a seaside resort from the late Victorian period until the mid-1950s. The photographs and their handwritten messages allow us to appreciate the town's significance as a favoured destination for people across the UK and beyond, a tradition now continuing through recent investment in our re-emerging tourist industry based on our stunning beaches and parks.

Caroline offers us an array of visitors to South Shields from 1901 to 1956, and although the language may have changed, the sentiments have not. Caroline presents the cards in such a tantalising way, begging the question 'what happened next?', and her geographical, rather than chronological, organisation of material is particularly helpful. She has also provided an invaluable insight into the hobby of postcard collecting, explaining classifications, commenting on design and market value and listing publishers and printers located in the town and abroad.

Sisters Gracie and Flossie salute 'Canny South Shields, Pride of the Tyne'. Caroline has indeed done justice to our town and I hope that this will be the first of many books from this gifted author.

Heather V. Thomas
January 2014

SECTION 1
OUTLYING AREAS

Westoe Village

Marsden Rock

SOUTH SHIELDS

West Park

The Pier

Terrace. South Marine Park

Westoe

A stunning aerial view of the Westoe area produced as a postcard by Aerofilms of London. The Ingham Infirmary, with its two grand lodges and impressive grounds, can be seen in the centre. St Michael's church is to the left of the view. Leafy, affluent Westoe Village, to the bottom right, has remained virtually unchanged over the years. Westoe Cricket Club was once a real village team. In 1868, the club leased a ploughed field from the church commissioners and members rolled and levelled it themselves. The first game played on the field was 'married men versus bachelors'. Shortly after the First World War, the site was bought for £2,500. The date on the Cricket Pavilion reads 1886. The postcard was sent from South Shields in 1919 to Nurse Lock, No. 5 Cromer Terrace, Leeds. The message reads, 'Have seen some very pretty places here! The pier is marvellous!' The card was published by R. Johnston & Son, Gateshead.

Westoe Village

These two postcards show the view down the village looking west towards Sunderland Road. Notice the castellated detail on the roof of the White House. There is another building in the grounds of the White House, the Gazebo, fronting onto Horsley Hill Road. When it was built, *c.* 1766, it had another window in the upper storey, which would have been used as a lookout point. There are several houses with these lookouts that would, at the time, have had a clear view over the harbour. The card below was produced by Ramsey, Sykes & Co., Laygate Lane, South Shields.

Westoe Village

Here are another two views looking down the village. Some of the impressive houses on the right include La Tourelle, the Briary, the White House and Sunny Lea. These were the properties of affluent merchants, land owners and ship owners, who could afford to breathe the air out of smoky, choking South Shields. Wyvestow Lodge's domed turret can just be seen. Westoe's old blacksmith's used to be on the site of Wyvestow Lodge before Sunderland Road split the village. The lichen-covered post between the railings is an opening to part of the ancient track known as 'Salters' Trod'. The panning of salt along the banks of the River Tyne could possibly date back to medieval times. The fish that was landed needed to be preserved and the salt pans produced the salt to do it. The salt would be packed up and carted away by horse for distribution, along well-worn tracks.

Westoe Village, South Shields.

Westoe Village

Printed in Germany and posted in Whitley Bay in the summer of 1910, this card shows the view towards Normanhurst. The White House can be seen behind the foliage. The gaudy colouring of Westoe Hall, below on the right, is true to the colouring of the plans for it. The hall's stabling and lodge are now stylish apartments. There were five other grand houses further east of the village: Stanhope House, Sylverton, Rockcliffe, Fairfield and Ingleside. The long, tree-lined driveway to Fairfield can still be seen and at the time of writing, the pillars of the lodge of Eastgarth still survive in Grosvenor Road.

Westoe,
South Shields.

THE CEMETERY. HARTON. (1149

Harton Village

Harton Cemetery opened in 1891 and covers an area of over 50 acres. The lodge and chapels are Grade II listed and are currently not at risk. Henry Grieves, the architect, designed them in a free, late Gothic manner, with Tudor overtones. Ordnance Survey maps of 1895 show the chapel on the left as Church of England and the one on the right as nonconformist. The grand frontage of Harton Hall can be seen in the card below. Mr Joseph Mason Moore, a solicitor in the town, made this his home for a time and loved his extensive gardens. Today, the hall has been developed into a small shopping area and residents of Moore Avenue share his grounds between them. St Peter's church can just be seen, along with the original Vigilant pub. This E. Johnston & Son card was posted in South Shields to Miss Brough in Stockton-on-Tees. The message is to the point, and reads, 'Arrived safe, send postcard tomorrow night, say how you are getting on, Father.'

HARTON HALL & VILLAGE. 1153.

Harton and Westoe

St Mary's Terrace still remains in the village today. The narrow lane that leads to the police station on Sunderland Road can be seen. Attractive housing has replaced the fields, farms and ponds and the rural feel to the village has diminished. Posted in South Shields, the card reads, 'Dear Lizzie, Nellie won't be coming up til Wed as Will caput her back Thursday. She will help me with the children a bit. Hope you are all well and Elsie is better.' Shield Laundry & Dye Works, of Osborne Avenue, advertise themselves as French cleaners. Their receiving offices in 1909 were at No. 69 Mile End Road and No. 23 Frederick Street and the telephone number was simply 149.

West Park

West Park was created in 1895 after South Shields Corporation bought 39 acres of farmland. The west area of the town was rapidly becoming built up and there was 'breathing space' needed for children to play. The elegant bandstand survives, a fine wrought-iron and honeyed wood structure. Harton Colliery Band played here in the summer of 1960 and included renditions of 'Colonel Bogey on Parade', closing with 'God Save the Queen.' Note the terraced housing in Stanhope Road, built in the 1890s. These two cards were never posted. The card above is a Valentine's Series and the one below was published by Ruddock Ltd of Newcastle upon Tyne.

West Park

A miniature golf course, bowling greens and tennis courts were once here for recreation in the park. In 1922, Dulcie sent the card above to her Daddy to wish him many happy returns on his birthday. He lived at No. 352 Stanhope Road, very close to West Park. The postcard below shows the leafy landscape and the lake, which drained the Brinkburn and gave rise to the name of Brinkburn Dene. Corney Field, Clover Field and Meadow Close were among some of the charming names associated with the area. A man of few words, Bert simply wrote, 'Don't you think this splendid?' Miss Martin in Boscombe, Bournemouth, was the recipient of the postcard.

Lake West Park So. Shields

Tyne Dock

This row of buildings in Slake Terrace is no longer there. The terrace was demolished to widen the road. From the right, the corner of J. S. Huntley, the grocer, can be seen, with Dunn's the butcher to the left. Next along is Maughan's dining rooms and then P. G. Watson, the grocer. Working left, the Banks o' the Tyne Inn can be seen, followed by the North Eastern Hotel and the Empress Hotel. Ward's Directories list other watering holes around the Slake Terrace area as the Dock Hotel (locally known as the 'Boodie Bar'), the Tyne Dock Hotel (now Kennedy's) and the Shakespeare Inn (known as 'the Shakey'). The tram is en route to the Market Place. The card below was posted to Hamburg in 1904, possibly by a seafarer.

Tyne Dock

Tyne Dock, the second busiest port in the country (second only to London), was officially opened in 1859. Allegedly, so many vessels crowded the dock in its heyday that it would have been possible to get from one side to the other, merely by stepping from deck to deck on the moored vessels. Below is a hand-coloured card showing the gates and warehouses at Tyne Dock. The view is down Hudson Street and the buildings on the left still remain as the premises of Harle Peel, bottled gas supplier. On the right, behind the policeman, is the Dock Hotel. The warehouses were well-known landmarks at Tyne Dock, built for the storage of grain in the 1880s. They became unsuitable for modern cargo handling and were demolished in 1964.

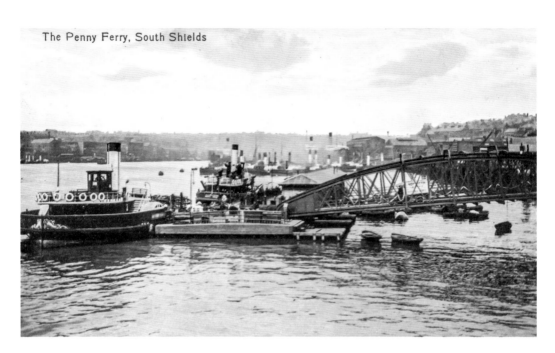

Ferries

There have been steam ferries between North and South Shields since 1827, run by various companies with varying success. These ferries were vital but unreliable and did not operate in the fog or at night. Today's ferries are the *Pride of the Tyne* and the *Spirit of the Tyne*. Between them they make just under 25,000 journeys a year, carrying around 400,000 passengers. The Valentine's card above was never posted, while the one below was used as a shopping list, the owner on his way to buy potatoes, milk, ham and bread. The coloured postcard shows the north side of the River Tyne, with Milburn Place and Smith's Docks in view, as well as the ferry *Northumberland*.

Penny Ferry, South Shields

Fishing Boats, So. Shields.

Fishing Boats and the TS *Wellesley*

These fishing boats, or cobles, are heading out to sea, passing the Pilot Jetty. The coble was a type of open, traditional fishing boat, which developed on our North East coast. The distinctive shape of the boat (flat-bottomed and high-bowed) arose to cope with the particular conditions prevalent in this area. Flat bottoms allowed launching from and landing upon shallow, sandy beaches, an advantage on this part of the coast, where the wide bays and coves provided little shelter from stormy weather. However, fishermen required high bows to sail in the dangerous North Sea and in particular to launch into the surf and land on the beaches. Ruddock Ltd was the producer of this card, which was never posted. The ship on the card below is the *Wellesley* training ship. The institution was established in 1868 by a group of philanthropic Tyneside businessmen 'to provide shelter for Tyneside waifs and to train young men for service in the Royal and Merchant Navies'. They initially used HMS *Cornwall*, but around 1874 took over an old wooden battleship, HMS *Boscawen*, which was renamed TS *Wellesley*.

WELLESLEY TRAINING SHIP. 450.
DESTROYED BY FIRE 11th MARCH 1914.

THE ROCKERY, CLEADON PARK, SOUTH SHIELDS.

Cleadon Park and Railway Station

This sepia postcard shows the rockery in the Dell, at Cleadon Park. The Dell was formed in the disused quarry at the top of Quarry Lane. A huge outcrop of rock there was known as 'Crow's Island', and who could forget the 'Cinderella' steps? In 2011, the park received a grant to plant new trees and replant the sad-looking flowerbeds. The card above was posted to Melbourne, Yorkshire, in the summer of 1946. Our beautiful Victorian railway station was designed by William Stocketon and built in 1879 by the London and North Eastern Railway (LNER). The Grade II listed building survived the bombing raids on the night of 9 April 1941. A shower of incendiaries fell on the Mile End Road, River Drive and Wapping Street area, as the attack concentrated mainly on the shipbuilding, ship repair and timber yards on the river. The station was hit but not destroyed. The trains were replaced by the Metro and the station fell into disrepair, finally being demolished in 1998. The tiled wall map, which was installed in 1905, survived and is housed safely in South Shields Museum.

SOUTH SHIELDS RAILWAY STATION.

Photo by Alex Drysdale

SECTION 2
DOWNTOWN

King Street

Two views, decades apart, looking from the Market Place down King Street. In the card above, Crofton's distinctive, friendly, family-owned emporium can be seen. Crofton's premises were at Nos 1, 2, 3 and 4 King Street and Nos 28, 29 and 30 Market Place, truly a large concern. Crofton girls worked from 8.45 a.m. until 7 p.m., and until 9 a.m. on Saturdays. Crofton's girls were not allowed to retain their jobs when they married. The premises were levelled by a German bomb during the Second World War. The South Shields crest is shown, with the legend 'Always Ready'. The writing on the card has faded but the publisher of the card is still visible, a South Shields business, J. Lawson & Son. En route to Tyne Dock is the No. 5 tram and the image contrasts well with the 'modern' motorbike in the card below, published for E. D. Walker & Wilson Ltd, Darlington.

King Street

Back in the 1800s, King Street was made up of a series of chambers, including Waterloo, Commercial, Wellington, Argyle, Albany, Union and Russell. The *South Shields Handbook* of 1936 contains advertisements for John Fenwick & Sons established in 1833, the 'complete house, hotel and ship furnishers'. Hogg Brothers could supply 'a good selection of novels, books of travel, guide books and maps, fountain pens and stationery'. The Golden Lion, a first-class family and commercial hotel, boasted a 'commanding position, a handsome Grill Room, table d'hôte luncheon, magnificent Banqueting Hall and Ball Room with Day & Night Porters'. Joures & Maltman proclaimed to be the largest draper's premises in the town in the 1920s. One of the stores was to be found on the corner of King Street. Below, a Raphael Tuck & Sons advertising postcard can be seen. These would have been delivered to wealthy ladies in the town. This one was posted to Mrs Sanderson of Ivy House, Westoe Village, in the early 1900s. *Ward's Directory* of 1901 shows her as being married to Mr William Sanderson, a marine engineer.

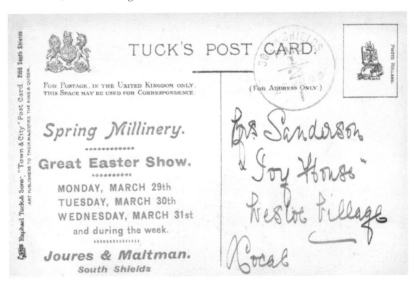

Ocean Road, South Shields

The Royal Hotel

Originally this was the Royal Commercial Hotel, then just the Royal Hotel and now the Ship and Royal. In the late nineteenth century, this establishment was taken over by Corbridge gentleman Farquhar Laing. He had ideas of grandeur and built a function room on waste ground to the rear of the hotel. The two were connected by overhead passages, the remains of which can still be seen today. In its day, this was the Royal Assembly Hall, an opulent Victorian society hall, later to become the Scala Cinema. Indeed, Queen Victoria stayed the night in this once sumptuous hotel. The fabulous card below may have been available to purchase at the hotel. There are various calculations on the reverse, all in pencil and in pounds, shillings and pence. Perhaps it was used to calculate a resident's bill.

OCEAN ROAD, SOUTH SHIELDS.

Ocean Road

The grand buildings in the black-and-white image mostly survive today, as a row of shops and bars. The fine building to the right of the lamp post was the Regent Hotel, which then became the Dorset Café and is now, at the time of writing, a bistro pub called Opal Lounge. The steeple of the Congregational church can be seen in both postcards. Thomas Masterman Winterbottom founded the Marine School over 150 years ago and it has been an integral part of cultural and economic life in the town for many years. Ocean Road had many terraces: Salmon, Hadrian, Gambetta, Garibaldi, Ocean, Pier and Glover, some of which still remain. Many businesses advertised themselves in the *South Shields Handbook* of 1936. Mason & Co. Ltd, No. 80 Ocean Road, provided 'bathing requisites, photographic supplies' and 'Sunbronze Oil'. Parker's restaurants, including the Mecca on Ocean Road, claimed to be the 'largest and oldest established seaside and provincial caterers'. Posted to Miss Alice Lauder, Old Station, Overtown, Scotland in 1904, Archie simply says 'Hope gran and all the rest of you are well.'

Ocean Road, showing Congregational Church, Marine School & Board School.   South Shields.

MUNICIPAL BUILDINGS, SOUTH SHIELDS. (998.)

Town Hall

South Shields is very lucky to have two town halls, an old one and a 'new' one. The story of the new town hall started with a competition for the best design for the new building. In 1902, plans submitted by London architect Ernest E. Fetch were finally accepted, for buildings to cost £45,000. Our 'new' town hall is a magnificent and prestigious building that has won many accolades over the years for its fine architecture and imposing style. It is a great source of local pride and an integral part of our heritage. We celebrated her centenary in style in 2010 with a spectacular light and sound show.

MUNICIPAL BUILDINGS, SOUTH SHIELDS. 1322.

Market Place and Old Town Hall

Our old town hall is Grade II listed but for a while the councillors wanted to raze it to the ground. Local people were understandably outraged, one of them calling it a 'pigeon's toilet'! In the end, the council decided by 42 votes to 13 to renovate it in 1976. The ancient door to the cells underneath still remains, and one of the cells has been converted into an office for the manager of the market. St Hilda's church, our oldest place of worship, can be seen in the background. It comprises an apsidal chancel, a nave, north and south porches and a western tower, containing a clock and a peal of eight bells. St Hilda's church continues to be at the very heart of the community in which it stands. The installation of a screen at the back of the church has meant the creation of a visitors' centre, a calling point for many pilgrims during the year.

Market Place, So. Shields.

27

Market Place and Old Town Hall

Our lively market continues to be popular three days a week, bringing people into the town to browse the many colourful stalls and grab a bargain! Crofton's corner is no longer, being all but destroyed in the Second World War and replaced with a concrete monstrosity. The Queen's Hotel can be seen to the left of the town hall in this hand-tinted card. Crofton's ornate building dominates the corner of King Street and the Market Place and was all but destroyed in the Second World War. It seems vehicles were allowed on the Market Place; the car on the right has the registration number CN 1911, indicating it was first registered in Gateshead. The 'CN' registration was used from December 1903 to November 1946.

SECTION 3
ALONG THE PROM

BATHING POOL, SOUTH SHIELDS

WOULDHAVE MEMORIAL AND LIFEBOAT, SOUTH SHIELDS.

219543

The Wouldhave Memorial and Lifeboat

On 28 May 1887, a meeting was held to consider suitable proposals to celebrate the Golden Jubilee of Queen Victoria. Twenty-eight entries were received to design a monumental tribute to the great William Wouldhave. The monument was to cost no more than £500 and J. H. Morton's design, made of sandstone, was favoured and later constructed by R. B. Farbridge. It was completed in 1890. The *Shields Gazette* of 18 June provided its readers with a full description: 'The design of the monument is massive and in keeping with the surroundings. The first stage is utilised as a fountain with surrounding basin 22 feet in diameter, the water supply being on the north and south sides from large shells placed in semi circular recesses. The water flows into the bowls and overflows again into the large basin.' William Wouldhave was born in Liddell Street on the north side of the River Tyne in North Shields. Later, his family moved across the water to South Shields; the reasons for doing so are not clear. He married a girl called Hannah and lived at Nelson's Bank at the Mill Dam.

LIFEBOAT TYNE

TYNE

4

OLD TYNE LIFEBOAT, SOUTH SHIELDS.

The Lifeboat *Tyne*

In January 1789, the brig *Adventure* of Newcastle was driven ashore in a horrendous gale, which would see eight of her crew drowned. Locals watched in horror as the despairing crew fought for their lives, but were unable to help. Soon, they would build the world's first purpose-built, successful rescue boat, now known as a lifeboat. As part of the 'Hello Tomorrow, Change is Happening' project, the lifeboat and canopy are being lovingly restored. The *Tyne* lifeboat has been restored at the North East Maritime Trust, which was set up by local enthusiasts in 2005. These cards show how railings and a planted garden surrounded the boat at one time. The Majestic Theatre and Ballroom was behind the Wouldhave Memorial at the Pier Head. Advertised as 'South Shields' Brightest Spot', it could be hired for meetings, theatrical performances, whist drives and functions of every description. In the 1930s, private dance classes were held in the ballroom by Madame Golledge.

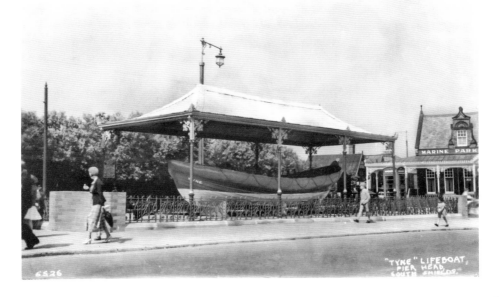

THE HARBOUR, SOUTH SHIELDS. (474)

The Harbour

A whole railway line of trucks, containing stone presumably quarried at the Trow, can be seen. The North Marine Park has not been laid out here and the stone may have been used as features in the park, as well as for building the piers. The hand-tinted card below shows the south pier, north pier and the lighthouse on the groyne. Many vessels are in the mouth of the River Tyne. The International Hotel in Belfast was its destination when it was posted in December 1913. To the right of this card is where we now have *Conversation Piece*, locally know as the 'Weebles'. Twenty-two bronze figures, each one nearly a quarter of a ton and a metre and a half tall, were created by Spanish sculptor Juan Muñoz.

Mouth of the Tyne, South Shields

VIEW FROM NORTH MARINE PARK, SOUTH SHIELDS

Caravan Park

With our beautiful coastline and rich heritage, it was inevitable that we would need a caravan park to accommodate our flocks of visitors during the booming era of the 1950s and '60s. These seem to be touring caravans. The site is now home to the Littlehaven Hotel, a fabulous conference centre and wedding venue with commanding views over the harbour. The view across the River Tyne shows North Shields and Tynemouth. Some people remember the saying, 'North Shields is the sunny side but South Shields is the money side.' This may have been true when South Shields was in its heyday at the turn of the century. In the card above, the Sir James Knott's memorial flats stand majestically on the top of a hill in Tynemouth. Building started in the 1930s and by 1938 they were nearing completion. They were probably the first ever flats built with special features to help tenants withstand air raids, essential with the gathering clouds of war. Two of the special features were the use of fire resistant materials throughout, unusual for those days, and the huge cellars designed as air-raid shelters. It was thought that these flats could have become a prime target for Nazi bombers as they stood on a high cliff overlooking the mouth of the Tyne, above the notorious Black Middens and looking out to the North Sea. In fact, each flat was designed to look out over the river or the sea, and the building would also become a notable landmark for sailors coming home to the river.

Caravan Site showing River Tyne, South Shields

Bathing Pool, South Shields.

Outdoor Bathing Pool

The very old outdoor swimming pool was on the North Foreshore. It opened in 1923 and proved very popular until just before the Second World War. The pool was 176 feet long (thirty lengths to the mile) and 50 feet wide. The depth varied from 3 feet 6 inches to 6 feet 6 inches. Seating was provided on the east and west sides to accommodate 1,000 spectators. From Monday to Saturday, the pool was open from 7 a.m. until dusk. Admission charges in 1936 were 3*d* each for spectators and bathers and you could even hire a towel and a costume! Catering facilities were provided and, depending on the temperature of the water, a hot drink or ice cream was on offer. The Verona Café, a branch of the Roma Café and Dairy, overlooked the pool and sold afternoon teas, chocolates and confectionery. Notice the ornate turrets and the castellated walls. The changing rooms for gents were at one end and ladies the other. Coincidentally, our latest swimming and leisure pool, Haven Point, has been built on almost the same site.

Bathing Pool, South Shields.

Flying and Skating

This terrifying amusement ride called 'Aerial Flight' was on the North Foreshore beside the Pier Head. Its hoarding reads, 'For all ages, passed and approved by authority. 1*d* for the flight or fright of your life?' The splendid white building below was situated around where the Sea Hotel car park is now and was the Olympia Skating Rink. The *Shields Gazette* of 31 October 1889 reported, 'A 2-mile amateur skating handicap took place in the rink on Monday night. There was a very large attendance of ladies and gentlemen from Nottingham, Sunderland, Newcastle, Tynemouth and the surrounding district. Dancing and skating were indulged in during the earlier part of the evening and at 8.15 the floor was cleared for racing. At 9.15 the final was started.' The prize for first place was a fine marble clock, the second place winner received a fancy timepiece and the third received a breakfast cruet.

Tynemouth from the Pier and Groyne

The postcard above was posted from North Shields to a Miss Piper, the Vicarage, Appledore, Devon. 'The weather has cleared up a bit so we have come to Tynemouth. It is a pretty seaside place. Love N.' Someone has written on the back of the card their idea of what may be happening in the scene: 'Barges would be loaded with rocks for pier repair. A tug would take the barges from the nearby jetty to be dumped at the south pier end.' This would seem to make sense. Below, the sepia card shows Tynemouth from the Groyne (notice the unfortunate spelling!). This is a view of the north side before the building of Knott's flats. It was posted from South Shields in the summer of 1930 to Mrs A. Thompson, No. 48 Church Street, Winlaton, Blaydon-on-Tyne. It simply reads, 'Got here alright'. It would seem that postcards were very much the forerunner of the text message. The stamp used is a King George V Penny Red.

TYNEMOUTH FROM THE GROIN, SOUTH SHIELDS.   2

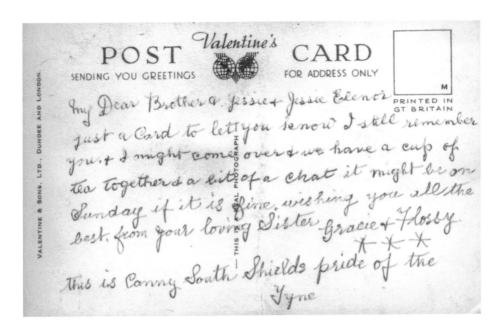

On the card, in handwriting:
My Dear Brother & Jessie + Jessie Elenor
just a Card to let you know I still remember
you, + I might come over & we have a cup of
tea together & a bit of a chat it might be on
Sunday if it is fine, wishing you all the
best, from your loving Sister Gracie + Flossy
✗ ✗ ✗
This is Canny South Shields pride of the
Tyne

VALENTINE & SONS, LTD., DUNDEE AND LONDON.

North Beach and Caravan Site

The sentiment on this Valentine's card is lovely: 'I might come over and have a cup of tea together and a bit of a chat.' The card has no stamp on it, so it may or may not have reached Gracie and Flossy's relatives. The front of the card is a sepia image that can be seen later in the book, showing the promenade with a view across to the funfair with its prominent helter-skelter. The M&L Series card below shows the sweep of the north beach, the caravan park in the distance and the high and low lights on the north side of the river. At the foot of North Marine Park, a row of cafés and shops can be seen. The shops were opened in 1924. There were shelters built on top of these and the views of the harbour must have been spectacular! The card below was posted to Mrs Hewison, No. 5 Rectory Lane, Winlaton. It reads, 'Dear Aunty Sally. I am enjoying myself a treat. Maggie had two donkey rides and made pot pies every day on the sands, with lots of love to Uncle Bob and Robby. From Sunny Jim.'

North Beach and Caravan Site, South Shields. 19

The Pier, South Shields

The Pier

The foundation stone for the pier at the mouth of the Tyne was laid on 15 June 1854 in the presence of the authorities from both sides of the river. It was finally completed in 1895. The pier is 130 feet short of a mile in length and is still a glorious walk on a sunny day. Note the steamer coming into the harbour on the R. Johnston & Son, Monarch Series postcard below, which was posted from South Shields to New York, USA.

Lighthouse, South Shields Pier.

The Pier

In January 1960, the Tyne Improvement Commission started a modernisation process to the pier and the foreshore. The M & L National Series card above was not posted and may have just been collected. Divers worked on the construction of the south pier and worked on the foundations, which were dug an astonishing 44 feet below the high water mark into boulder clay and shale. The card below was penned in the gardens of Ford Castle in Berwick-upon-Tweed and sent to Mr Savage in Humshaugh, Northumberland.

THE LIGHTHOUSE, SOUTH SHIELDS.

The Pier

Exactly the same postcards! The one below has been colour tinted. The 80-year-old Titan crane spent most of its working life dropping 40-ton blocks of concrete to provide a protective arc for the pier against the rough North Sea. The crane was sold to a Yorkshire firm and ended its days as scrap metal. The hand-tinted card below was sent in 1904 to Miss Straker in Wimbledon Park, Surrey. It reads, 'I heard from Edward, he is feeling better at school now. I am going to write to him today as I owe him a letter. Have you managed to eat all the cakes yet? Much love from JB.'

South Shields. The Pier.

thanks so much for post-card. I am so glad you like the "There is it". I will write you a letter next Sunday. J. Grazier

The Pier

In June 1919, applications were received from J. Bird, R. Woodhouse, J. G. Mitchelson and J. B. Johnson for permission to use the steps and slip along the north side of the pier for passengers getting on and off their pleasure boats. Tyne Improvement Commission agreed to charge them all 2s 6d each for the summer season. The old Titan crane can be seen in the top right of the postcard. It was used in the construction of the pier, carrying a superstructure of concrete and built stonework. The Valentine's card above was posted to Harrogate by Arthur. 'Having a nice time here and having glorious weather. Give my love to dad. Hope you are all A1!' The legend of the 'dolly' in the lighthouse is still told today. One of the stories told is that a keen fisherman found a child's doll in the street on his way to fish on the pier. When he arrived, some of the cement of the newly built lighthouse was still wet and on the spur of the moment he pushed it in!

THE PIER AND LIGHTHOUSE, SOUTH SHIELDS.

The Pier

The Tyne Improvement Commissioners helped to make the Tyne one of the finest ports on the North East coast. Back in the 1860s, the commissioners oversaw major dredging operations, which deepened the river substantially and enabled much larger vessels to ease into deep, safe waters. By the early 1930s, more than 160 million tons of material had been dredged and taken out to sea. The treacherous sandbar at the mouth of the river was gradually dredged away and the Tyne was widened and straightened. Then the enormous task of constructing the piers began. Like two protective arms, the piers made our river one of the most important harbours of refuge on the North East coast for vessels in distress or sheltering from stormy seas. The card below reads, 'Dear Mother, just a few lines, Lizzie and I have been here today. It had to snow but it was better than rain. I have had a lovely time, it has flown over. I will be home tomorrow. I wrote to May on Sunday and then went off to a big party! Will give you all the news later. So goodbye, hope you are quite well. From Harriett xxxxx.'

PIER AND LIGHTHOUSE, SOUTH SHIELDS.

86. THE PIER, SOUTH SHIELDS

Life Brigade House

Here are two views of the Life Brigade House, situated on the pier. Every day since 30 January 1866, twenty-four hours a day, 365 days a year, South Shields Volunteer Life Brigade has stood ready to help those in peril around our shores. One of the wrecks in the first year of the brigade's service record occurred in 1866, when the schooner *Blossom* came ashore on the south beach. A total of ninety-eight men and three officers answered the call and the crew of three were safely landed by breeches buoy. Neither of these cards was posted and the card above simply reads, 'This is the commencement of the pier.'

Fishing on the Pier

This fabulous postcard shows dozens of boys in their best clothes on the pier with their fishing rods, hoping for a bite! Lawe Road can be seen behind the newly planted North Marine Park, and the South Marine Park with Seaview Terrace is to the left of the Life Brigade House. The local Jude's Art series card was posted in 1905 to Mr and Mrs Shiel in Guildford, Surrey. One thing that has become apparent when researching is that many cards were written with the message upside down. Was it to stop the postman reading it on his rounds? This is a typical example posted in the summer of 1905 by Lillie. She was staying with a relative, a Mrs Allen in Saville Street.

Section 4
MARINE PARKS & THE SEAFRONT

South Marine Park

Opened in 1890, South Marine Park is probably the finest example of a traditional Victorian park in South Tyneside. Borough Engineer Matthew Hall produced the design and a suitable park keeper/gardener was sought. Mr John Peebles of York was formally appointed in July 1886 and so he could be close to his work he lived along the way in Salmon Street. A special attraction of the park was the annual illuminations in the first two weeks of September. Known as the 'illuminations', there would be open-air dancing, band performances, illuminated waterfalls, floodlighting and fireworks. Posted in South Shields in 1956, this card reads, 'We are in the North Marine Park at present. Weather is lovely. We are in with the Murton Old People's trip. 25 bus loads! Love from Gran and Grandpa.'

Bandstand, South Park, South Shields.

The Bandstand, South Marine Park

The *Shields Gazette* hailed the new bandstand as 'one of the prettiest in the North of England'. In August 1904, Lt Amers' Military Band performed at the opening ceremony. Over 12,000 people turned up for the evening concert and kept coming back for more in subsequent years. In 2008, the South Marine Park was restored to its Victorian splendour along with the bandstand. The card above was printed in Bavaria and not posted.

IN SOUTH MARINE PARK, SOUTH SHIELDS. H.9086.

South Marine Park and Lake

During the First World War, a 'Dig for Victory' campaign led Mr Bennett to plant potatoes in the park. Mr Bennett was Mr Peebles' successor as head gardener. Towards the end of the war, he was delighted that he had harvested 2 tons in this latest crop. The lake in the postcard below originally had two islands in it, and the Ordnance Survey map of South Shields 1894–96 shows them both. One still remains but the other one, to the south, was removed in the years following the First World War.

MARINE PARK, SOUTH SHIELDS.

10721.H.

South Marine Park and Lake

This postcard was posted to Southampton. Seaview Terrace and Seafield Terrace are very distinctive and have changed little over the years. A few years ago, a mummified cat was found in the porch foundations of one of the houses in Seafield Terrace. It has been kept as a lucky charm. In the card below, families are enjoying the lakeside. On the right you can see the boathouse. The park's model yacht club is one of the oldest in the country, and at one time 'gentlemen' hired professional skippers to sail their boats. The council minutes of 1893 state that Mr T. T. Anderson submitted a letter on behalf of the yacht sailors urging the removal of the small island from the lake. Presumably, it was difficult to manoeuvre their craft around. The island is no longer there.

Marine Park, South Shields

Grand Promenade

Taken from the grand promenade looking towards the boating lake, these postcards are of a similar view. The formally laid out walkways were very popular with nannies and their charges. Some of the terraces were deliberately constructed to be wide enough for a horse and carriage to traverse. It was a way for park visitors to take in the sea air without having to leave their carriage. The views over the harbour are second to none.

South Marine Park

These cards were posted in 1905 and show a similar view. The Wouldhave Memorial (correctly titled the Jubilee Memorial) is clearly visible, as is the ornate Marine Parks Restaurant. The postcard above shows the South Shields crest and motto in 1850. In the centre of the card below, Mr Peebles' greenhouses can be seen, along with the ornate Victorian rain shelter to the right of the Marine Parks Restaurant. At the instigation of Alderman Gompertz, the South Shields Corporation converted the shelter into a small community theatre to mitigate the loss of the Queen's Theatre, which was destroyed by bombing in the Second World War. The Pier Pavilion was opened on Whit Monday 1949 and for the next few years presented seasons of repertory and concert shows. Nowadays, the Westovians theatre group regularly perform plays and farces to packed houses.

South Marine Park, South Shields

North Marine Park

This is the view down the north park and up the south park to Beach Road. The four detached, grand houses remain and have been extended sympathetically and interspersed with newer town houses. You can also see the Wouldhave Memorial and the bandstand. The card above was posted to Mr F. Brown, the Sneap, Greenhaugh, Bellingham. It reads, 'My dear son, hoping you are a good boy and letting the cat have a rest. Tell Aunt Mabel to be a good girl now I am not there to look after her. Best Love, Daddy.' On the card below there are bowlers on the greens wearing suits and flat caps, ready to take their shots. Their bowls or woods would probably be made of lignum vitae. The Marine Bowling Club was known as the 'Mother Club', being the oldest club in the town, closely followed by the Borough Bowling Club. The Marine Club had a member of the Readhead family as president for the first fifty years.

CHILDREN'S PLAYGROUND, NORTH MARINE PARK, SOUTH SHIELDS.   2/9595

North Marine Park

In the earliest days, the North Marine Park was well stocked with wild animals and birds. There was a fishpond, an aviary containing British and foreign birds and a peacock and hen that would strut about. A silver fox was housed in a rock-covered dugout, which later became a tool house near the bowling green. There was also a tame raven and a porcupine that lived in the yard to the rear of the park superintendent's house. The *Gazette* of 26 May 1893 reports, 'The porcupine, the disappearance of which from the North Marine Park and the ineffectual attempt at capture among the rocks near the breakwater, that created such a sensation in the town, has been captured. It was discovered at about 20 past twelve in the morning by PC Wilson, making its way along Stanhope Road at Tyne Dock, evidently bent on taking a passage by some outward bound vessel from these inhospitable shores. The officer succeeded, without a revolver, in driving it into an empty house and lassooed it with a piece of string and drove it before him in triumph, to the Tyne Dock Police Station where it was accommodated with quarters. It was subsequently handed over to the Park authorities.'

SOUTH SHIELDS. THE LAWE NORTH AND SOUTH MARINE PARKS.

53

North Marine Park

The remains of this archway are still visible in the park today. Three friends pose underneath the arch, which has now been removed for health and safety reasons. The rocks were probably hewn from Trow Quarry and feature prominently both in the North and South Marine Parks. The sepia card above was never posted and is from the Excel Series. Mrs J. Lincoln of Poole, Dorset, was the recipient of the card below, posted in South Shields in September 1928. It reads, 'We are having a lovely time and I do love Jim and Will. I saw nice little babies today, the lady says I can bring it home, love Jack.'

South Shields.

North Marine Park

Posted in 1909, this postcard shows the ornate bandstand that is no longer there. Curiously, there was a bandstand in the North Park before one was erected in the South Park. To the left, St Aidan's church can be seen, sadly no longer there either. The park superintendent's house, with its distinctive chimneys, can be seen on both cards. Trinity Towers can also be seen on the card above. A traditional game of putt can still be played on the same site today.

North Marine Park, South Shields 15

PROMENADE TENNIS COURTS AND PIER, SOUTH SHIELDS.

Promenade from North Marine Park

Plenty of hard and grass tennis courts were available in the town. Tennis players in their whites can be seen on the postcard above. Our newly completed promenade/sea wall at Littlehaven has been built on almost the same site. The Valentine's card made its way from sunny South Shields to Apeldoorn, in Holland.

PROMENADE AND BEACH, FROM MARINE PARK, SOUTH SHIELDS.

Long Sands, South Shields

Bowling Greens

'Can you find me in the crowd here?' reads this Valentine's card, posted to Mr Halcrow in Ravenglass, Cumberland, in 1903. In the early 1930s, a team called the 'Sand Dabs' could be seen playing 'friendlies' in the North Marine Park. The team was made up of Tyne Pilots.

North Marine Park

Never posted, this postcard shows the newly constructed, grand North Marine Park overlooking the busy harbour. The card was phototyped in Berlin and has a divided back to accommodate both the message and the addressee's name and address. This type of card was introduced in Britain in 1902. The postcard below is a view towards Tynemouth and four steam tugs can be seen. Some tugs of the time include the *Charles Dickens*, the *Bon Accord* and the *Lady Tredegar*.

TYNEMOUTH FROM NORTH MARINE PARK, SOUTH SHIELDS.

Fun on the North Beach

Fairground attractions sprang up on the north beach many years before the Dunes Amusement Park was created. With swing or 'shuggy' boats, circus rides and donkeys, there were also pleasure boat trips around the harbour and out between the piers. On the right are the ticket huts for pleasure boat trips, including Mitchelson's and Thompson's. In the 1940s, there was an exotic zoo hidden in the fairground. Two lions were caged there, along with a couple of black bears, monkeys and an alligator. The card below was posted from Kirkby Stephen to a Miss Rhodes in Piercebridge. It shows how smoky the harbour could get.

The Sands

The Valentine series of postcards is very collectable. These two sepia cards were never posted and show our beautiful, sweeping beaches. People seemed to make going to the beach a real family day out, sometimes even taking a full Sunday lunch along. Children and adults alike take to the sea. The men are wearing suits and flat caps, which was a common occurrence in the day.

North Sands

It may not have the high profile of Blackpool or the lure of the Costas, but on a good summer's day, people can be seen enjoying one of the best coastal stretches in the country. These postcards had no destination and were just collected and treasured. Interestingly, a collector of sand samples is called an arenophile. Apparently, there is an International Standard that categorises sand as a material consisting of particles between 0.063 mm and 2.0 mm in diameter. Any finer and it's classed as coarse silt and any larger and it's fine gravel.

THE PROMENADE, SOUTH SHIELDS.

The Promenade

The south promenade was first opened in 1927 at a cost of over £50,000. Ordnance Survey maps show that initially it ran to what is now the Sand Dancer pub, but was then extended towards Trow Rocks. For a time, this area was renowned for the delights of Frankie's Ritz Café, where you could always get hot water to make your tea on the beach. The Valentine's card above was posted to Brampton in 1959 and reads 'Having a nice time, we have been here two days running (our shoes will need resoling). Molly is sunbathing, the weather is lovely. Love Molly, Len and Doris xxxx.' Notice the ornate balustrading is still a work in progress.

The Beach looking North, South Shields. (6a)

THE PROMENADE CHALETS, SOUTH SHIELDS

Promenade Chalets

After 1918, beach tents were replaced with lean-to huts and marquees that served as public shelters. The huts were probably predecessors of the present-day chalets. People would take along chairs, mattresses and cooking utensils to make them more comfortable. The accommodation is now known as Sandhaven Beach Chalets. Vastly improved, they are self contained, double glazed and can sleep up to five holidaymakers comfortably. Positioned slightly back from Sandhaven Beach, the chalets are always popular with holidaymakers throughout the summer. The lovely sentiment on the card below made its way to Cumberland in 1910. It tells of the sheer delight and squealing of a child who had probably never seen or felt sand before.

Fun at the Beach

As well as our beautiful beaches, South Shields has always had a sense of fun. We now have a dedicated funfair and have come a long way from the 'shuggy boats' and 'Pierrot shows', however quaint they were. Today, this area is home to the Dunes Amusement Arcade. Slightly to the right of this view is now home to the Blue Marlin, selling traditional, fresh fish and chips! Smuggler's Cove is another addition to our expanding holiday seafront. It offers a thrilling game of crazy golf, played to the theme tune of *Pirates of the Caribbean.* A few ponies are saddled, waiting patiently, ready to trot along the beach at Sandhaven Beach.

FRENCHMAN'S BAY. So. SHIELDS

Frenchman's Bay

This beautiful bay derives its name, as Richardson's Terrier of Survey tells us, from a French ship wrecked there many years ago. In the early 1900s, the bay was home to an eccentric character called 'Willie the Rover'. He built himself a primitive hut on a level platform at the end of the bay. A large coastal defence battery was constructed at Frenchman's Point, above the bay. The work on the battery or fort began in 1900 and was maintained with varying armament as part of the Tyne defences until 1943. The site was later partially demolished and landscaped and now forms part of the Leas area. Frenchman's Bay Holiday Camp was near the famous Marsden Rock and offered every accommodation, including a field for sports, bathing, boating, fishing, football, cricket and dancing. Sunday schools, Boy Scouts, Girl Guides and cycling clubs were all catered for at moderate prices. There was even a good car park and a garage! To book early and avoid disappointment, Mr G. B. Wilson, Fort House, should have been contacted by telephoning South Shields 1204.

FRENCHMAN'S BAY, SOUTH SHIELDS. 1323.

Trow Rocks

A lovely coloured postcard of the 'Nest', which was built on Trow Lea. This quaint, thatched cottage was home to the first onsite foreman for the building of the south pier. There were quite a few of this type of cottage, put up by the workers. Stone for the pier was quarried at the Trow and transported by rail along to the Pier Head. The Nest was quite close to the boundary stone, which can still be seen at the side of the road running down to the car park. The headland of Trow Rocks has always been an important defensive position for the Tyne area and has seen various military installations over the years, including the 'disappearing' gun that recoiled into a pit once fired.

SECTION 5
MARSDEN BAY
& GROTTO

Marsden, Rock, South Shields.

SOUTH SHIELDS. MARSDEN GROTTO.

Marsden Grotto

The history of Marsden Grotto is steeped in the colourful, bygone days of cruel seas and hardened smugglers. 'Jack the Blaster' was first to live in the cave. He moved to Marsden Village on the clifftops in 1872, to work in the local quarry. Castellated walls were very much in vogue in South Shields, as can be seen throughout the postcard collection.

THE GROTTO MARSDEN, SOUTH SHIELDS.

Marsden Grotto

These images are very early and obviously before the lift shaft was added! This meant the roughly hewn, steep steps were the only hazardous way down to the sweeping bay. The postcard, *carte postale*, *Postkarte* or *briefkaart* below was sent to 'Kit' as a reminder of building 'sandcastles' in 1905.

Marsden Grotto.   Near South Shields.

I cannot give you the exact spot but not far from here. It

Hills. Sunderland.

Marsden Grotto
These postcards show the 'Marine Grotto', an alternative name for Marsden Grotto. The lift is totally exposed to the elements and looks quite terrifying compared to the safe brick structure we know today.

Marsden Grotto

A few decades ago, there was a charge made to use the lift. A commissionaire sat upon a high stool and charged coppers to ride down the cliff face. A menu from the Grotto in the 1970s boasts Duck a l'Orange at a pricey £1.15 and Fillet Steak Rossini at £1.40. If you really wanted to push the boat out, a bottle of Moët et Chandon was £3.20. Happy days! Atop the cliffs, Marsden Village can be seen. The original community was born as a result of sinking the colliery pit shaft in the 1870s. There was only a handful of streets with miners' cottages in this temperance village, perched on the clifftops to the north of Souter Lighthouse.

Marsden Grotto

Renowned for being the only restaurant and bar in a cave in the whole of Europe, these postcards show the ancient ballroom as being very basically furnished. Legends of smugglers, wrecks and colourful characters abound. The Monarch postcard below was not posted and the one above was posted in 1934. 'We've spent today here and it's lovely but very rough.' Not sure if it was the clientele or the weather?

The Ancient Ballroom, Marsden Grotto. 13124.

Hermits' Bar and Smuggler's Lair Entrance

The ghost of John the Jibber, who died a long and lingering death suspended in a coal bucket halfway down the cliff face after betraying fellow smugglers to the customs men, is said to haunt this ballroom. Many people bought South Shields' own fast-selling board game, 'Grotto Ghost'. Three hundred games were sold in only three days at the Flower Show in Bents Park in 1977! At £1.50, it was a bargain and people sent them to friends and family across the globe.

M 1   THE BUFFET ENTRANCE TO SMUGGLER'S LAIR, MARINE GROTTO, MARSDEN.

Marsden Rock

Over the years, the mighty North Sea has fashioned the coastline into dramatic cliffs and bays, with sea stacks and caves to explore throughout the year. Rugged and weatherbeaten, Marsden Rock is one of the major tourist magnets in the town. Standing grandly in front of Marsden Grotto, the 100-foot-high rock is home to one of the most interesting seabird colonies on the North East coast. Thousands of pairs of fulmars, kittiwakes and cormorants can be spotted nesting there. The rock and the Leas are now protected by the National Trust.

Marsden Rock and Cliffs, South Shields

Marsden Rock

These similar views not only show the magnificent, much-loved Marsden Rock, but also the other magnesium limestone sea stacks, of which some remain as our coastline slowly erodes. Some of the famous limestone stacks include Pompey's Pillar, Lot's Wife and Jack Rock. These two cards show the erosion of the same stack, which is no longer there today. The postage for the card above was ½*d* inland or 1*d* to send abroad.

Marsden Rock and Grotto, South Shields

MARSDEN BEACH, NEAR SOUTH SHIELDS.

Marsden Bay

Long before the package holiday arrived, folk from all over the country would visit our glorious beaches. A tent could be hired for a small fee. The tidal island off the north end of the bay is known as the Velvet Beds, so called because of the fine, springy grass and thrift that used to flourish there. The more common name is Camel Island, now that it is bare and its shape resembles such a beast.

MARSDEN BAY, SOUTH SHIELDS.

G.5480.

Marsden Bay

The card above is a collectable Valentine's card, posted in 1954. It reads, 'Dear Ivy and Syd, Having a lovely time, have been to Sunderland, Newcastle and Whitley Bay already. Been swimming and dancing several times. It is marvellous scenery around here and the train ride up last Saturday was terrific. Love Derek.' Simple pleasures.

Marsden Rock and Grotto, South Shields

THE GROTTO, MARSDEN, NEAR SOUTH SHIELDS.

Marsden Bay

This sepia Excel series postcard shows families enjoying themselves at Marsden Bay. The children are happily digging and playing in the sand while their mothers relax. Before the addition of the lift shaft, the only way to get beer barrels down to the pub premises was to winch them down via the wooden platform jutting out over the Grotto pub. The foundations for the supports can still be seen from the Grotto car park. Below is another view of mighty Marsden Rock; this time, the wooden steps or ladders erected by Peter Allan during his time at Marsden can be seen. Allegedly, the first lady to set foot on the top of the rock was Julia Collinson of Gateshead. Later, in 1908, there was a mighty choral service on the rock by combined choirs, with flags, bunting and banners waving.

SECTION 6
NOVELTY CARDS

Multiview Postcards

The collecting of postcards is known officially as deltiology. Here are a few novelty cards from the collection. With just one of these cards, you could show your folks a lot of views of sunny South Shields and give them a flavour of your travels. The card above is interesting as it shows hand-coloured images on a banner. It also bears the South Shields Crest ('Courage, Humanity and Commerce'). Snowdrops show a promise of spring in the 'sepia-tone' card below.

Multiview Postcards

This lucky black cat has pride of place in the centre of this card. He is surrounded by more great views of our seafront and town hall. Below, pastel roses surround some quaint hand-tinted and embossed views on this Lilywhite card. Bob sent this card to his Auntie Nellie. 'Got here in good time, love Bob.' Short and sweet.

Multiview Postcards

Typical multiview cards boasted the best views of the town. Our glorious Victorian parks, beautiful bays and ornate buildings all make for a pleasing selection of sepia and coloured cards. Mr McCarthy of Wallsend was the recipient of the card above. 'Just a card to remind you that you are not forgotten. Will come and see you when the fine weather comes. Love from Ethel.'

Multiview Postcards

Mabel sent this postcard to Flo in Heaton in April 1914, before the start of the First World War. They made arrangements to meet each other in the Central station in Newcastle upon Tyne. The Valentine's card below was posted to Burton upon Trent and the family had 'beautiful weather, Charles took the news very well, returning a week today'. I wonder what the news could have been?

Just for Fun
By changing the name in the caption, comic cards of this type could be sold at different holiday resorts. Holidays at the seaside became more affordable and popular during the Victorian era, thanks to the expanding railway network. For the first time, resort towns were within reach of ordinary families. Many postcards were bought and sent home to family and friends. The cute Florence Valter cat and kitten card was posted in the summer of 1948. Auntie Mabel posted it to her niece, Miss Ella Gentle, in Hertfordshire.

Good Luck all the Way from SOUTH SHIELDS

1812   Florence E. Valter.

84

Lift our Heads up and you'll find
Why this place should be kept in mind

1397

Pull-out Postcards
A pull-out postcard had a small flap as part of the design, perhaps as a postman's bag, or, in this case, the donkeys. The flap could be lifted to reveal a strip of tiny views folded concertina-style below it. Neither the cute beach donkeys nor the crab were posted and maybe stayed in a child's collection.

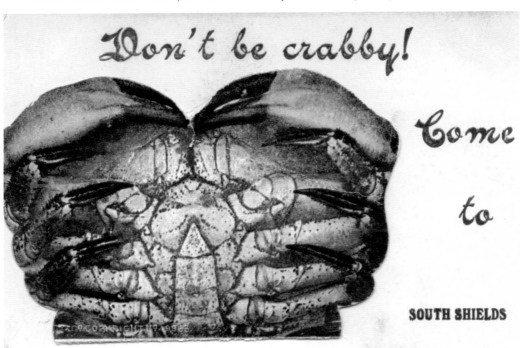

Don't be crabby!

Come

to

SOUTH SHIELDS

Left by the Tide at South Shields.

Novelty Postcards

This cute child poses for the photographer in an enormous seashell (presumably not a real one). It was posted in South Shields in the summer of 1910. The seashell postcard reads, 'Dear mother and father. I arrived safely, Katie and Lily had been at the station from about 7 o'clock.' The beach donkeys were once a familiar sight on the north beach. Under their furry coats is a concertina of twelve black-and-white vistas of our spectacular seafront.

Two's company three's none at SOUTH SHIELDS

I'M SIMPLY CARRIED AWAY BY THE CHARMS OF SOUTH SHIELDS

Novelty Postcards

Humour is to the fore with this cartoon of a beach donkey, heavily laden with a bouncy lass, galloping along the beach – a true flavour of summer! Below is a curious card, posted to Jesmond in 1908, with a pair of sweethearts framed in a kipper! The word 'giddy' means frivolous or light-hearted.

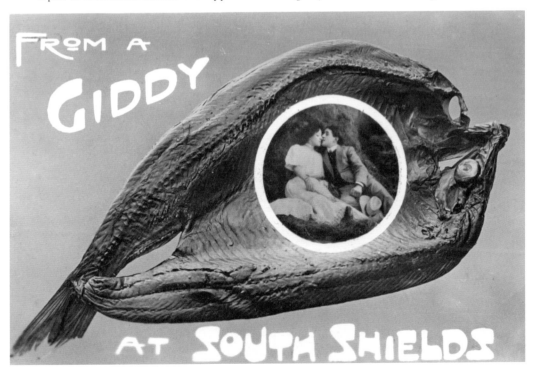

FROM A GIDDY AT SOUTH SHIELDS

Good Luck from **SOUTH SHIELDS**

1996

Pull-out Postcards

This Valentine's 'Mail Novelty' postcard was posted from South Shields to Richmond. 'Dear Ken and Colin, we are having lovely weather. We are sitting in the sun today. Don't forget your duties. Will write later on in the week again, love mam and dad xx.' These cute Scottie dogs hide a concertina of a dozen tiny black-and-white images of our stunning scenery. The card below assures friends and relatives that all is well during the war. The flap on the balloon covers the usual folded vistas of the town.

We are Keeping a Good Look-out at SOUTH SHIELDS

Don't let this give you all a fright,
Just look inside it—We're all right.

1336

SECTION 7
MAPS

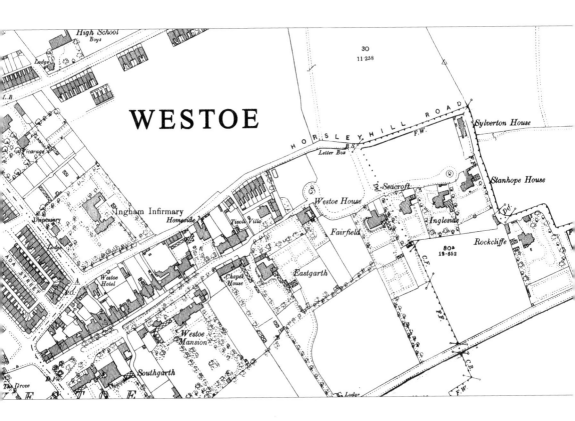

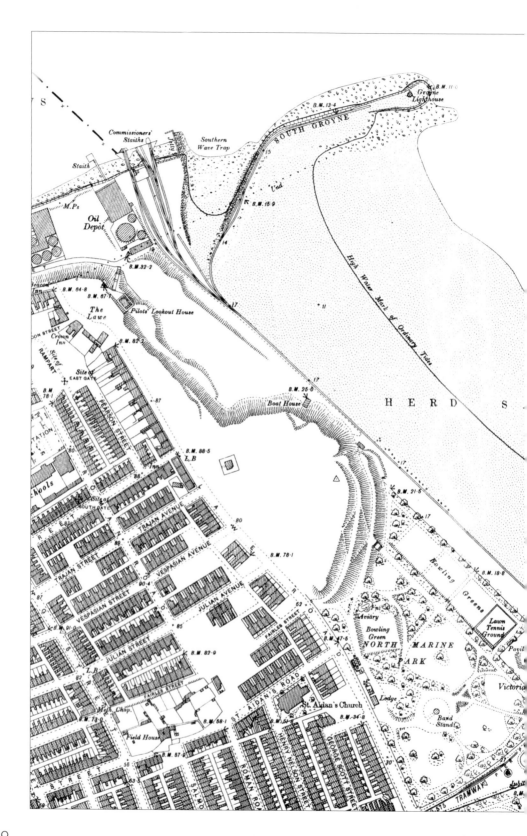

UTH SHIELDS

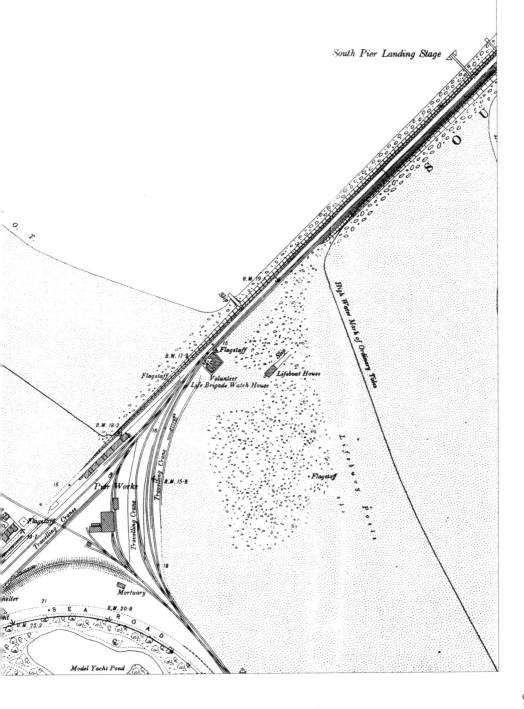

South Pier Landing Stage

SOU

O. T.

B.M. 19

Slip

High Water Mark of Ordinary Tide

B.M. 17·9

16

Flagstaff

Slip

Flagstaff

Volunteer
Life Brigade Watch House

Lifeboat House

B.M. 18·2

16

Lifebuoy Pools

Flagstaff

Travelling Crane

B.M. 15·8

Flagstaff Crane

16

Pier Works

19·2

Travelling Crane

18

Mortuary

helter

21

SEA ROAD

B.M. 20·8

nt

B.M. 25·2

Model Yacht Pond

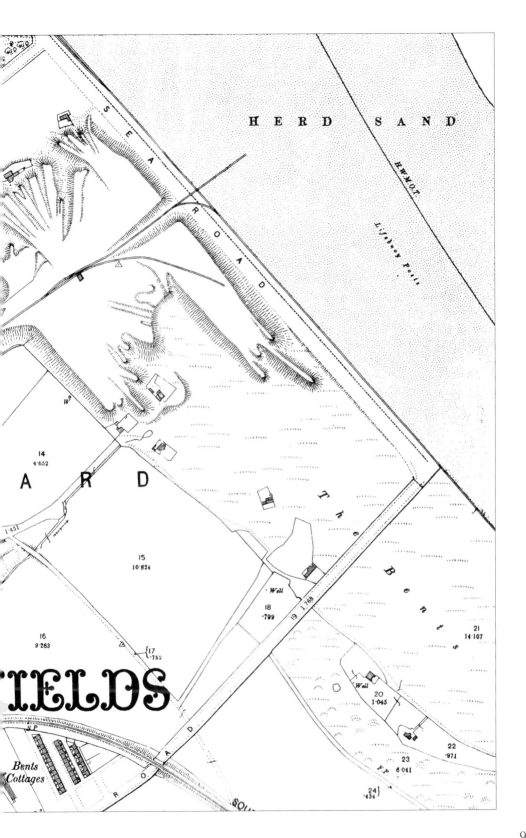

HERD SAND

H.W.M.O.T.

Lifebuoy Posts

SEA ROAD

△

W°

14
4·652

A R D

·451

15
10·824

The Bents

18
·799

Well

19 1·758

16
9·263

△

{17
·752

21
14·107

FIELDS

Well

20
1·045

S.P

22
·971

Bents
Cottages

23
6·041

R O A D

FP

24
·434

SOU

95

SOURCES & ACKNOWLEDGEMENTS

The archive material in South Tyneside Central Library has proved an indispensable resource for this publication. The collection of *Shields Gazette* cuttings in South Tyneside Library was an enormous help, and *Ward's Directories* from 1890 onwards were useful in sourcing names of shops and pubs. Paul Usherwood's book, *Public Sculpture of North-East England* (South Tyneside Bowling Association, 1892–1992), provided a number of useful facts.

THE AUTHOR

Caroline Barnsley was born and has lived in South Shields all of her life. Working in South Tyneside Libraries for over thirty years, latterly in the Local Studies and Heritage Department, she is passionate about South Shields and is herself a descendant of a long line of Tyne Pilots. Caroline lives with her family, minutes from the coast that she loves. This is her first book.